Wolfgang Paul Costanza

Stock market speculation
made easy

AF176485

Publishing house:
Books on Demand
Norderstedt, Germany
ISBN9783752823455
© 2018 Wolfgang Paul
Costanza
Cover: Sculpture before the
Frankfurt Stock Exchange from
the sculptor Dachlauer
Photo: Wolfgang Paul Costanza

Table of contents

Introduction

A common prejudice:

Success on the stock market requires extensive knowledge and a lot of work and time. As a result some investors do not invest in shares, even though they generate the most profits over the long term.

The reality looks happily different:

For the stock market success only two conditions are required: Some basics and the knowledge of the three best equity strategies developed by the most successful stock market speculators.

Readers will learn through this book how they can acquire a large fortune with the help of the three best equity strategies.

The best speculators

Dear friend,

in your letter you asked me what arguments speak for the stock market. First I write what speaks against them:

The stock market has a female article in most languages and is a capricious, completely unpredictable lady. Sometimes she has a good mood, in the stock market language 'bull market'. Sometimes she is very distressed, in the stock market language 'bearish market'. She is heavily influenced by political events, even if they happen on the other side of the globe. She is always curious about positive and negative rumours, to which she responds with rising and falling prices.

If you want to do business with this capricious lady you have an advantage as a woman. Statistics prove that women on the stock market are on average more successful than men, as they prefer safe investment strategies, but men risk speculation.

Instead of boring you with a treatise on the methods of stock market speculation, I prefer to tell you the success story of the two best speculators:

Benjamin Graham was born in London in 1894. His family emigrated to New York. At the age of 20, Benjamin began his career on Wall Street. For 12 dollars a week he wrote stock prices on a blackboard. At the age of 25, he already had yearly income of 600 000 dollars. In 1934, he explained his new investment strategy in his bestseller *Security Analysis*. Taking this strategy into account, in 1948 he invested a quarter of his assets in the insurance company '*Geico*'. Over the next 8 years, he made a 1635 % profit from this investment. For 30 years, his strategy has yielded an

average annual profit of 17 %.
10 000 dollars became 1 110 000
dollars. From 1928 to 1957 he
taught at *Columbia University*. There
was only one student to whom he
gave the best grade A+: **Warren
Buffett**. He bought the first three
shares at the age of 11. From 1945
he speculated in the investment
company of his teacher *Benjamin
Graham*. When he finished, *Warren
Buffett* raised 105 000 dollars from
his relatives and started his own
investment firm. This achieved an
average annual return of 29,5 %
from 1956 - 1969. 10 000 dollars
became 150 000 dollars. The relatives of *Warren Buffet* became
multimillionaires. In 1998, everyone
who had invested 10 000 dollars in
1956 had the fantastic sum of 150
million dollars. *Warren Buffet* has
acquired 75 billion in asset speculation. The share of its *Berkshire
Hathaway* investment currently costs
300 000 dollars and is the world's

most expensive share. *Warren Buffett* uses only the phone for its stock market speculation. He does not use a personal computer, because he has no interest in the current courses.

"I could also be somewhere where the post arrives three weeks late and invest wonderfully."

Unlike other famous speculators *Warren Buffett* makes no secret of his stock purchases. They are published and commented by him. This made him a guru for millions of small investors in America. These repeat his share purchases, which increases their price.

Warren Buffett has no high opinion of the Wall Street pros:

"Wall Street is the only place where people drive up taking the Rolls-Royce to ask the advice of people taking the subway."

With a fortune of 75 billion dollars, *Warren Buffett* is one of the five richest men in the world. Nevertheless, he still lives in the same house in Omaha, which he acquired in 1958 for 31 000 dollars. As a frugal billionaire, he bought his private plane at a bargain price. He rides a mid-range car and treats himself to a good meal at the steakhouse once a week.

In an interview with US magazine *'Fortune'*, on June 25, 2006, he announced that he would donate 85 % of his fortune to charitable organisations and medical research, 30 billion dollars of which to his friend *Bill Gates' foundation.*

Why did I tell you these success stories? They illustrate better than a stock market seminar: The most effective method of stock market speculation is to pursue with patience a good investment strategy.

Now I have to correct the negative image that I have designed by the stock market. The stock market is not only a fickle lady but also a great benefactress, as the life story of *Warren Buffett* proves.

Perhaps this letter has aroused in you the desire to also become a charitable millionaire, following the example of *Warren Buffett*. In another letter I will give you more information about the strategy of *Warren Buffett*.

To make you aware that you are in the best company as a speculator, I will introduce you to some prominent speculators:

The roman philosopher *Cicero* acquired by the real estate speculation a considerable fortune. He came to two findings that have kept their validity until today: money is the basis of the republic and speculation is the springboard to a great fortune.

The French writer *Voltaire*, a passionate speculator, had all the lots of the French state lottery bought up by straw men. He had calculated that the sum of the lottery winnings was considerably larger than the total price for the purchase of all lots. He was very rich by this coup, but the lottery director was dismissed without notice.

Other famous speculators: the painter *Gauguin*, the writers *Balzac* and *Beaumarchais* and the English economist *Lord Keynes*. Below his portrait, the British Government wrote the following text:

'*John Maynard Lord Keynes*, who managed to make a fortune without to work.'

Since I am doing a tour of *California*, you cannot reach me in the next four weeks.

The biggest stock market crash

Dear friend,

during your *California* trip, I read a book about the biggest stock market crash. It became clear to me: the stock market is not just that benevolent lady you've introduced to me. She has two faces: a friendly one that has shown her to *Benjamin Graham* and *Warren Buffett* and an unfriendly one that has shown her to many stockbrokers. One of them wrote: 'On the stock market you can make a small fortune by investing a great fortune.'

The stock market has repeatedly destroyed gigantic sums of money. In 1929, *Wall Street* caused the worst financial debacle in history. Before 1929, the world experienced the biggest stock market boom of all time. The speculative fever has infected all social layers. Hot share tips were even more in demand than the alcohol prohibited by the *Prohibition*. The chauffeurs only listened with one ear to the traffic; with the other they tried to catch a stock market tip of their passengers. The valet of a speculator won a quarter of a million dollars with the tip of his master. The stock market tip of a grateful patient brought 30 000 dollars to a nurse. The women urged their men to hurry so they would not be late in the race for wealth.

An actress adorned her apartment with graphs of rising share prices: *General Electric* rose 300 % in one year and *Radio Corporation* 400 %.

J. Raskop, director of *General Motors*, wrote in the *Ladies Home Journal*:

'Since income can be actually being increased in this way, I firmly believe that not only everyone can become rich but everyone is committed to it.'

God's own country was struck by the delusion that the abolition of poverty is imminent and then a new era of 'eternal prosperity' begins.

On October 24, 1929, the so-called **Black Friday**, began the largest financial debacle in history. The whole drama is illustrated by the course of the *Dow-Jones-Index*: At the first listing in 1896, the index has 41 points. Until 1927 he rises to 100 points. Through an overheated, partly bank financed stock market speculation, the index reached in September 1929 the record high of 381 points. The dizzy share prices are far above the real value of the companies.

Irving Fisher, a professor at *Yale University*, said on October 16:

"It looks like the shares have reached a permanent high plateau."

In the next three days there will be a crash of the stock market. The *Dow-Jones-Index* loses 15 %. On October 23, the index drops to 300 points. The following day, the **Black Friday**, the total value of all companies listed on Wall Street falls by 11 billion dollars. On Monday the index drops to 260 points. On Tuesday he lost another 12 %. On 15 November he drops to 180 points. In the summer of 1932, after a total loss of 89 %, he finally falls on the 41 points he had of the first day of his listing.

The share prices of the big American companies plunge into the abyss: *General Motors* from 73 to 8, *Radio Corporation* from 115 to 3 1/2, *General Electric* from 220 to 20.

In American statistics, the stock market crash is reflected as follows:

More than 123 000 successful speculators holding a luxury car had to transfer to the subway. As a result of the financial debacle, more than 9000 banks declared bankruptcy. The American legend of rag, which rises to the millionaire, played out more and more often in the opposite direction. Millions of shareholders in America and Europe were destitute, but struggled to find rich people to beg for.

Finally I tell you two anecdotes:

The son of a stockbroker asks his father:

"You're always talking about *bull market* and *bear market*. What's that?"

"I'll explain that to you with examples, son. *Bull market* means luxury cars, champagne and fantastic women. *Bear market* means subway, Coca Cola and your mother."

The American comedian *Will Rogers* had sold all shares before the biggest stock market crash. The rising number of suicides inspired him to the following gag:

'In New York, the hotel porter asks new arrivals: Do you want a room to sleep or jump out of the window?'

I care a lot about sleeping well. Therefore, I cannot decide to join the club of shareholders, which consists mainly of risk-taking men.

The safety net of the smart investor

Dear friend,

upon my return from *California*, I found your letter, which I answer immediately.

The crash of the *Dow-Jones-Index* between 1929 and 1932 to the value of 1896 shook your confidence in the stock market. I can understand that well. However, the further development of the *Dow-Jones-Index* is a success story:

In1954 he reached the level of 1929 again. In 1972 he broke through the sound barrier of 1000 points. In 1987 he climbs over 2000 points. In 1992 he clears the hurdle of 3000 points. Thereafter, he rises to more than 26 000 points by 2018. Although the price increase was repeatedly interrupted by stock market crashes, the *Dow-Jones-Index* raised a lot from 1896 to 2018.

Stock market boom and stock

market crash are two sides of the same coin. The stockbroker *André Kostolany* writes:

'No stock market crash that was not preceded by a boom and no boom that does not end with a stock market crash.'

A speculator said:

"There is no ringing before the crash."

However, there is an alarm signal before the stock market crash: the so-called *Housewife's stock market*. This means that people are entering the stock market speculation, which have no idea about stocks. The American billionaire *John Rockefeller* obviously had a keen sense for this warning sign. He sold all the shares a few weeks ago *Black Friday*, as a bootblack had given him several share tips.

Due to the experience of the *Black Friday*, the stock exchanges set a new rule to prevent an avalanche-like sell off. In extreme price losses, trading is suspended on the stock market. Thanks to this strategy, none of the later stock market crashes had more the devastating consequences than the *Black Friday*.

After the stock market crash of 1987, the Frankfurt stockbrokers proved that they had not lost their humour. They wrote the following text:

My finances are shattered.
It crashed on the stock market.
I got that from my shares
made kites to children.
I went with them to field,
where the breezes blow gently.
There I was able to see my shares
go up again.

Perhaps I can give you back the lost confidence in the stock market by introducing you the DAX yield triangle of the *German Stock Institute*. This return triangle proves that the DAX index stock has always made a profit when there is a long interval between buying and selling. For example, from 1983 to 2006 the average annual profit was 10,7 %. Only short intervals between buying and selling led to losses, for example, between 2002 and 2004, to an average annual loss of 6, 2 %.

The triangle consists of 300 fields. The blue fields mean wins, the red fields mean loss and the white fields mean a yield of 0 %. 87 % of the fields are profit fields. Only 10 % of the fields are loss fields.

I hope the small number of loss fields will give you again confidence in the stock market.

One can compare the stock speculator with a tightrope walker. If he falls, his life is saved by the safety net. If the speculator was smart enough to build a safety net, his fortune will be largely salvaged in the event of a market crash.

The speculator *André Kostolany* has the opinion:

A stockbroker, who does not bankrupt at least twice during his career, is not a real speculator. In my view, he is a bad speculator. The good speculator protects him through a *safety net* consisting of the following 7 rules:

1. Invest only part of your assets in shares. The share of the securities portfolio is calculated according to the following formula:

Share in % = 100 minus age.

A 25-year-old should therefore invest no more than 75 % in shares. For a 75-year-old, the share may only be 25 %.

2. Buy stocks only with money you do not need over a long period of time. If you need the money a short time later, you may have to sell the shares at a loss.

3. Invest your money in different shares from different industries. This reduces the price risk.

4. Invest your stock gains into fixed income securities. When the returns

are reinvested in stocks, and when there is a stock market crash thereafter, most of the gains are lost. However, when the gains have invested in fixed income securities, they remain. For the stockbroker it is hard to turn stock gains into safe securities with low interest rates. That's why *André Kostolany* writes:

'It is not difficult to make money. It's hard to retain the money.'

5. Realize the equity gains. One should always remember: the stock market is not a one-way street. Gains are only borrowed money that you have to repay at the next price loss. When you realize a profit by selling shares and switching them to safe securities, the profits are retained. If the price continues to rise after the partial sale, the investor can be pleased as the shares remaining in the portfolio continue to rise. And he can be satisfied if the price falls after the partial sale, because he has put part of the profit

on the safe side in time.

6. Never buy shares with the help of bank loans. In a stock market crash, the loans cannot be repaid. However, the repayment claim of the bank remains. The investor is in dept.

7. Minimize your losses by selling the shares as soon as possible in the event of a price loss. A proven exchange rule is:

Let price gains run, keeping price losses small. To compensate for a loss of 50 %, a price increase of 100 % is required.

To lighten up my stock market seminar, I'll tell you a few anecdotes:

Ms *Pollak of Parnegg*, the wife of an ennobled Viennese textile industrialist, was famous all over Austria for her style flowers.

She sends her son a telegram:

'Morning evening concert. Please come.'

The son telegraphs:

'Not possible. Lie with *influenza* in bed.'

Answer telegram from the *Baroness:*

'Give her 100 crowns and send her away.'

After the concert, the *Baroness* radiantly approaches the pianist and says:

"I've already heard *Arthur Rubinstein* ..."

The pianist bows flattered.

"I have already heard the magician *Franz Liszt* ..."

The pianist bows even deeper. The *Baroness* ends her sentence:

"Neither of them sweated like you."

After the evening, the *Baroness* says to the *Princess of Esterhazy*:

"At my next concert, I want to offer something very special to the guests. Can you give me a hint, Your Highness?"

"I say only one word: *Roséquartet.* Your guests will be amazed."

One month later, the two women

meet in the *Burgtheater*.
The *Baroness* to the P*rincess*:

"Strange man, this Mr *Rosé quartet*. Although I hired him alone, he brought along three other people."
I owe the music an important insight about the stock market. Just as the success of a piece of music depends on just a few notes of the melody, the stock market success is based on a few basics.

The basics of stock market trading

Dear friend,

I am glad that you want to enter the stock market speculation because of my letter. However, you must first learn the basics of stock market trading. After that you can make big profits through the stock market. You write:

'I have no idea about stocks.'

According to a survey, half of all Germans regarding equities are unsuspecting. Therefore, the share of shareholders in Germany in 2016 was only 6 % (France 15 %, Switzerland 20 %, Great Britain 23 % and USA 25 %).

Germans have a savings of 5100 billion Euros. But only 6 % of them have shares. However, the shares earn more profit in the long run than any other investment. The average return on equities over the past 50 years has been 2 % above the average rate of return on fixed income securities. In a short investment period, this interest difference has little effect on profit. In the long term, however, the yield gap due to compound interest is very large. The final amount of a 9 % return investment exceeds the final amount of a 7 % return investment by 40 % in 10 years, by 173 % in 20 years and by 565 % in 30 years.

The stock market is an important engine of the economy. The financiers (shareholders) and the money recipients (entrepreneurs) meet here. The entrepreneurs increase their capital by transforming their company into a stock corporation. Shareholders can benefit from company profit distributions and rising share prices.

By purchasing a share, the investor becomes the co-owner of the company. He is involved in the profit, if the development of the enterprise is good and at the loss, if the development is bad.

A **stock index** is made up of a larger number of shares. The 100 largest English stock corporations form the FTSE100, the 30 largest American companies the *Dow-Jones-Index* and the 30 largest German stock corporations the *German Stock Index* (abbreviation DAX).

ETF (Exchange Traded Fund) is a fund that reflects the performance of a stock market index. Example: An ETF based on the *Dow-Jones-Index* reflects as closely as possible the price of that index. The value of the ETF is 1/100 or 1/10 of the index value. If the *Dow-Jones-Index* is 26 000 points, the value of the ETF is 260 or 2600 dollars.

The ETF offer the opportunity to invest in all the stocks of an index by buying only one security.

The ETFs are traded on the stock exchange and can therefore be bought or sold at any time.

Due to its passive management, the costs are much lower than in the case of an actively managed fund.

The dividends are either distributed to the fund owners or reinvested in the fund.

The ETFs are treated as special assets. In the event of insolvency of the issuer, they remain the property of the investor.

When buying a share, you either give the order to buy the cheapest price or you name the price you want to pay the maximum. When selling you either give the order to sell at the highest price or you name the price you want to receive at least.

When building a stock package, there are two options. You can buy an equal number of shares every month, or you can spend an equal amount of money every month to buy stocks. I recommend you the second option. If you spend an equal amount on shares each month, fewer shares are bought each month in the case of rising prices, but more shares in the case of falling prices. As a result, a cheaper purchase prise than the acquisition of an equal number of shares per month.

Because of his sometimes somewhat puzzling statements *Warren Buffet* was nicknamed '*The oracle of Omaha*'. However, he gives a clear answer to the question of the best time for stock purchases. In his opinion, most shareholders make the mistake of being too influenced by the rise and fall of stock prices.

"They feel good when their shares rise and bad when they fall. I feel good when the price of my share falls, because I can buy more shares."

Strongly believing that the shares he selects will rise in the long run, he seizes the opportunity of falling prices to buy these shares several times at ever-lower prices. He sets a price limit each time to achieve a lower average purchase price.

It is also beneficial if you buy a share shortly before the dividend distribution. The portion of the profit that a company distributes to its shareholders is called '*dividend*'. The calculation of the dividend yield is very simple:

Dividend yield in % = dividend divided by share price x 100.

The dividend will be distributed the day after the General Meeting. Any shareholder who has a share in his depository on the day of the General Meeting will receive the dividend. The day after the dividend payment, the share price will decrease by an amount equal to the dividend.

I will now explain to you the most important causal factors for the development of share prices:

The relationship between supply and demand determines the share price. Increasing demand has a positive effect on the share price; falling demand has a negative effect. Here, the economic situation plays an important role. This runs in 4 phases:

Economic upturn, boom, downturn and recession.

In the economic upturn and boom investors can buy more shares because of their rising income. Share prices rise. In periods of economic downturn and recession, investors can spend less money on shares. Share prices are falling.

An important causative factor in rising prices is a falling oil price. Since investors have to spend less money on energy costs (gasoline, heating), they can buy more shares.

An important causative factor in falling prices is an increase in interest rates of fixed income securities. In this case, investors will buy more fixed income securities and therefore have less money to buy shares.

You have now learned the basics of stock market trading. Apart from this basic knowledge you only need to know the three best stock market strategies in order to make big profits on the stock market. I will introduce you these strategies in my next letter.

Finally, two anecdotes about *Baroness Pollak of Parnegg:*

The couple *Parnegg* dine in a restaurant on the outskirts of Vienna. A gentleman sitting at the next table introduces himself:

"Baroness, my name is *'Prochaska'*. This name means 'walk'."

After dessert, the baroness winks at her neighbour and says:

"Come with me to the park. Let's do a little *'Prochaska'* together."

One day, the *Baron of Parnegg* suddenly disappeared. You look for him in the office, with all friends, acquaintances and relatives, but in vain: He remains untraceable. The *Baroness* always has the best ideas in the bed. So she decides to lie down in bed to think again about where her husband might be. In the bedroom, she suddenly sees under the bed a black shoe and, as she bends, the pale face of her dead husband. She rings the maid and says very annoyed:

"Look, Lena, how you tidy up."

.

The three best strategies

Dear friend,

at a carnival session in Mainz the cabaret artist *Herbert Bonnewitz* joked:

"Dear Lady, whom let you think for you?"

Regarding stock speculation, you should have no inhibitions to let the stock market professionals think for you. It is better to make a lot of money with their help than by speculating on the stock market with little success. I will introduce you to the three best stock market strategies so you know how your future stock market profits will be generated. Stock picking with the three best strategies takes a lot of time and effort. That's why you'd better leave them to the stock market specialists.

The **value strategy** developed by *Benjamin Graham* is based on the following consideration:

If the stock market value of a share is lower than its real value, this share is bought over the medium term as investors recognize the under-valuation. Consequently, the price of this share rises. Due to the undervaluation, the risk of a price loss is low. The shares selected with the help of the 'value strategy' thus have a good price opportunity and at the same time a low price risk.

The MSCI EMU VALUE index reflects the performance of under-valued European companies. This index rose 95 % from 1997 to 2009. The index of companies that were not undervalued only rose 51 % in the same period. The difference of 44 % proves the superiority of the value strategy.

Determining the real value of a share requires a lot of time and effort. *Warren Buffett* employs a large number of people with this difficult task. That's why I recommend you buy an ETF fund based on the value strategy, for example:

UBS EFT MSCI EMU VALUE – A EUR DIS

ISIN: LU 0446734369.

The **dividend strategy** developed by *Benjamin Graham* is based on the following consideration:

The total return of a share consists of the price gain and the dividend. Shares that pay a high dividend therefore also have an above-average total return. There are two variants of the 'dividend strategy':

The strategy top 10

At the beginning of the year, you buy the 10 stocks of an index that pay out the highest dividend. These stocks are then kept in the depository for one year.

The low 5 strategy

Of the 10 stocks with the highest dividend yield, you buy the 5 stocks with the lowest purchase price. These are held for one year in the depository.

The 10 highest dividend shares in the *Dow-Jones-Index* returned an average annual return of 17 % from 1976 to 1996. The low 5 strategy returned 20 % over the same period. Both strategies outperformed the average annual return of all US shares, which was 11 %.

From 1974 to 1995, the top 10 dividend - shares in the DAX achieved an average annual return of 15 %, outperforming the average return of all DAX shares at 7 %. The Low 5 strategy achieved an average annual return of 20% from 1982 to 1996, surpassing the DAX by 8%.

The so-called DIVDAX is an index of the 15 DAX shares with the highest dividend distribution.

Between 2000 and 2011, the total return of the DIVDAX exceeded the total return of the DAX by 45 %. That's why I recommend you buy an ETF fund based on the dividend strategy, for example:

ISHARES DIVDAX UCITS ETF - EUR DIS

ISIN: DE 0002635273.

The principle of **momentum strategy** is to buy shares that are already on an uptrend. This upward trend can be seen from the fact that the share price has risen above-average in the last six month. The strategy is based on the following consideration:

If the share price has risen above average in the past, it is very likely to rise in the near future. When the price of share has risen, it tends to go up further. This dynamics of the course is called ‚momentum‘.

The stock market analyst **Robert A. Levy** developed a simple method to find shares with above-average price performance:

For all shares in an index, the average price of the last 26 weeks is calculated. Then you divide the current weekly price by the calculated average price of the last

26 weeks. This gives you a number greater than 1 if the current price is above the average price of the last 26 weeks, or less than 1 if lower. This number is called *Levy relative strength* (LRS).

The *momentum strategy* can be used with any index. When applied to the Dow-Jones-Index, a ranking of all shares in the index is created according to the LRS value. The 10 stocks with the highest LRS value are bought and held in the depository for one year.

The effectiveness of the *momentum strategy* was proved by calculations of the *University of Mannheim*: with this method, yields can be achieved that are 10 % above the average return of the index.

This method confirms the saying of British stockbrokers:

'The trend is your friend.'

I recommend you to buy an ETF fund based on the *momentum strategy*.

Finally, I tell you an anecdote about

the Berlin banker *Carl Fürstenberg*:

He had received a compartment in the first class of the sleeping car due to highest protection for the journey from Warsaw to Berlin. As the train left, Mr L. approached him, whom the banker had just met at a business dinner at the hotel Adlon.

"Mister Fürstenberg, I just see that your second bed is vacant. I'll pay you any price if you leave it to me."

At that moment, Furstenberg remembered that Mr L. had eaten noisily, which caused him to associate an even loader snore. Thoughtfully, he looked at Mr L. and said:

"I'll sleep on your proposal."

When the train stopped at the border station the next morning, he woke up with the squealing of the braking wheels. He heard the cutting voice of the customs officer:

"Border station, passport control."

Tired and pale, Mr L. sat on his suitcase.

Fürstenberg said:

"If I see you like this, I'm sorry afterwards that I did not offer you my second bed."

Mr L. answered:

"The night was not so bad; but the worst part is that the customs officer reproached me because yesterday I forgot to pick up my passport at the hotel reception. I could not get this stubborn official by my requests nor by a dizzy high bribe to let me enter Germany."

At that moment, the stubborn official left a neighboring compartment. The banker went to him and said a few words. Then the official came to Mr L. and tapped his service cap:

"You can enter Germany."

Mr L. would like to have the banker around his neck. He went to him and squeezed his hand with great gratitude.

44

"Thank you very much, Mister Fürstenberg, but what did you say to this stubborn Prussian official?"

"I gave him an official order and he said:
Of course, if you give me an official order."

The most common mistakes of shareholders

Dear friend,

before you go into the stock market speculation, I have to warn you the most common mistakes that are made by the shareholders. I have already introduced you to the safety net of the 7 rules. Unfortunately, these are ignored by most shareholders. In a booming stock market, stockbrokers tend to overweight the equity holding in their depository. This happens either because they do not know the formula: 'Share in % = 100 minus age' or deliberately disregard this formula.

A common stock market trap is a 'sure-fire secret tip'. Here there is a risk that other shares are sold in order to be able to put as much capital as possible on the one card of the sure-fire tip. If the sure-fire tip proves to be a flop, it means a significant loss for investors.

Few shareholders convert their equity gains into fixed income securities. They fear the threat of yield reduction when switching to fixed income securities. They do not understand that this yield reduction is the unavoidable price for securing their stock profits.

The *counter-cyclical strategy* is to buy at falling prices and sell when prices rise. Since the shareholder follows the herd instinct, it is difficult for him to sell with rising prices. If everyone buys, why should he sell against the tide?

However, there is a behaviour that is even more difficult for him: to sell a share whose price has fallen below the purchase price. This is interpreted by the shareholder in the sense that the purchase was a mistake. No shareholder likes to admit that he made a mistake. That's why he's looking for arguments not to sell shares, for example:

'The stock market was wrong and will correct this mistake again.'

As a rule, it is not the stock market that was wrong, but the speculator.

Another argument:

'It is a temporary price weakness, which is soon compensated by a rise in price.'

As stock prices sometimes recover on a declining share price, these price recoveries keep raising hopes for loss compensation. Accompanied by ever new hopes of the shareholder on a loss compensation, the share price drops to ever lower levels.

Another argument:

'As long as I do not sell the share, the price loss is not yet realized. Only when I sell the share will the loss be realized.'

If you do not sell a share that falls below your purchase price, you will be doubly damaging: Firstly, because of the loss of this share and secondly because of the lost profits you would have made if you sold the share early and invested it into a profitable share.

If a share falls 10 - 15 % below the buy price, I recommend that you sell the share.

In his book 'Geld, das große Abenteuer: Aufzeichnungen eines Börsianers' *André Kostolany* describes how difficult that is:

'The hardest thing is to accept a loss on the stock exchange resigning. It is a surgical procedure.

You have to amputate the arm before the poisoning spreads, the sooner the better. This is difficult and among 100 people there is only one who is capable of doing so.'

In all likelihood, you are not among the people who have the power to perform such an amputation. That's why I recommend you give your bank a *stop / limit order.* This means, on the one hand, that the share will be sold automatically if it falls below the selling price you set and, on the other hand, that the sale will only be made if the price is above a limit that you specify.

You can see how difficult it is for the shareholder to sell a stock that has fallen below the purchase price. However, there is a behaviour that is even harder for him: to buy sinking shares. Few have the power to buy shares when the entire stock market crashes. Again, the herd instinct proves to be the greatest obstacle. If one hears the call "fire" and sees all shareholders rushing to the stock exchange exit, one must have the steel-hard nerves of *Warren Buffet*, in order to remain in the stock exchange and to buy the shares, which panic sell the shareholders at rock-bottom prices.

André Kostolany describes the ups and

downs on the stock market as follows:

The stock market professionals ('strong hands') buy their shares in a stock market crash at rock-bottom prices. The stock market boom following the crash is increasingly attracting amateurs ('shaky hands') to the stock market. The stock market professionals sell these amateurs their shares during the stock market boom to maximum prices. The crash following the stock market boom throws the amateurs in a state of panic. They sell their shares, which they have bought at the highest prices from the professionals, back to the professionals, but this time at rock-bottom prices. After that, the game begins again, in which the amateurs always lose by paying the winnings of the professionals, who are always the profiteers.

Finally, I'll tell you an anecdote about a man who owed his biggest stock market coup to the panic of the stock market traders. He was a descendant of that legendary money dynasty which received the honorary title: 'Bankers of the Kings' and 'Kings of Bankers'.

Nathan Rothschild bought war bonds on the London Stock Exchange which financed England's fight against Napoleon. On June 18, 1815, there was a decisive battle at *Waterloo* between the troops of Napoleon and the armies of the allies England and Prussia. It is believed that the banker received the news of England's victory by a carrier pigeon of his Belgian agent.

He went straight to the Stock Exchange and sold his war bonds with a deeply depressed countenance. Panic-stricken, stockbrokers followed his lead and sold off their war bonds, which crashed in no time. The war bonds were bought by banker's straw men at rock-bottom prices.

A few hours later, the news of Napoleon's defeat led to a rally in prices on the London Stock Exchange. Biggest winner of the day was *Nathan Rothschild*. The panic of the stock market traders had him given the fantastic profit of one million in pounds sterling.